Acknowledgment

Images by CC0 public domain, these and other photos
can be found at www.pixabay.com

Wikipedia

copyright Ethel May 2016

# **Tigers.**

Tigers are the largest of the wild cat family. They are easily recognized by their orange/red background with black striped fur. The underneath of their bodies are lighter in colour. The largest wild tiger on record is over Ft 11 long and weight 857 pounds.

The tigers closest relatives were previously thought to be the lion, leopard and jaguar. However it is now believed to be the snow leopard.

# Tiger.

Tigers can be found in Bhutan, India, Nepal and Bangladesh.

They have long tails, large heads and the front of their bodies have powerful forelimbs. The pattern is different for each individual tiger. This pattern is also on the skin, so that if the tiger was shaved of its fur, the pattern would remain.

The tiger comes is various sizes, unlike others in the big cat family.

# White Tigers.

The white tiger is a variant of the Bengal tiger. The lighter colouring is a result of a lack of pigmentation. These white tigers have been observed in the wild in India.

It has become apparent that the white tiger is larger and heavier than their orange Bengal counterpart. They are therefore bigger at birth as well.

As with all tigers, their pattern is unique to them alone. It's the equivalent to the human fingerprint.

A variant of the lack of pigmentation in some white tigers, is so severe that they appear white.

White tigers outside of India and inbred. This inbreeding is often between brothers and sisters, and has led to the resulting tigers being cross eyed.

## **<u>Tiger wannabe's</u>**

These gorgeous tiger wannabe's really believed they are true tigers, and so proud of themselves.

The lesson here being we can all be whoever we want to be, we just have to believe.